A Book of Love for

MY
SON

A Book of Love for

MY SON

H. Jackson Brown, Jr., and Hy Brett

RUTLEDGE HILL PRESS®

Nashville, Tennessee

A THOMAS NELSON COMPANY

Published by Rutledge Hill Press, a Thomas Nelson Company, P.O. Box 141000, Nashville, Tennessee 37214.

Pages 14 center, 233, 240 bottom, 249 top, and 298 bottom, from *The Little Book of Big Questions* by Dianna Booher. Copyright © 1999 by Dianna Booher. Used by permission of J. Countryman, a division of Thomas Nelson.

Pages 20–21, 209 (adapted), and 312 (adapted), from *When God Whispers Your Name* by Max Lucado. Copyright © 1994, 1999 by Max Lucado. Published by Word Publishing, Nashville, Tennessee. All rights reserved.

Pages 46–47, adapted from "A Child No More" by Margaret Chittenden. Copyright © 1974 by Margaret Chittenden. Used by permission.

Page 51, "Work in Progress" by Barbara Brett. Copyright © 2000 by Barbara Brett. Used by permission.

Page 59, adapted from *This Is Your Time* by Michael W. Smith. Copyright © 2000 by Michael W. Smith. Published by Thomas Nelson, Inc. Used by permission. Michael W. Smith adapted the story from "Holy Fear: God Rules!" by Craig Cabaniss, published in *Sovereign Grace,* January/February 1999, 4.

Pages 93 and 236, adapted from *Closing the Gap* by Todd Duncan. Copyright © 2000 by Todd Duncan. Used by permission of J. Countryman, a division of Thomas Nelson.

Pages 207 top, 225 (adapted), 245 bottom, 263 center, 292 top, and 296 top, from *Something to Smile About* by Zig Ziglar. Copyright © 1997 by Zig Ziglar Corporation. Published by Thomas Nelson, Inc. Used by permission.

Page 227, from *Gates of the House: The New Union Prayer Book.* Copyright © 1976 by Central Conference of American Rabbis, New York, and Union of Liberal and Progressive Synagogues, London. Used by permission.

Pages 260–261, adapted from *Prayer: My Soul's Adventure with God* by Robert H. Schuller. Copyright © 1995 by Robert H. Schuller. Published by Thomas Nelson, Inc. Used by permission.

Cover and text design by Gore Studio Inc.

Library of Congress Cataloging in Publication Data

A book of love for my son / [compiled by] H. Jackson Brown, Jr. and Hy Brett
    p. cm.
    ISBN 1-55853-865-8
    1. Conduct of life—Quotations, maxims, etc. I. Brown, H. Jackson, 1940– II. Brett, Hy.

PN6084.C556 B65 2001
082—dc21

2001019028

Printed in the United States of America

1 2 3 4 5 6 7 8 9—06 05 04 03 02 01

CONTENTS

Other Books by H. Jackson Brown, Jr.

A Father's Book of Wisdom

P.S. I Love You

Life's Little Instruction Book™ (volumes I, II, and III)

Live and Learn and Pass It On (volumes I, II, and III)

Wit and Wisdom from the Peanut Butter Gang

The Little Book of Christmas Joys (with Rosemary C. Brown and Kathy Peel)

A Hero in Every Heart (with Robyn Spizman)

Life's Little Treasure Books

   On Marriage and Family, On Wisdom, On Joy,

   On Success, On Love, On Parenting, Of Christmas Memories,

   Of Christmas Traditions, On Hope, On Friendship, On Fathers,

   On Mothers, On Things That Really Matter, On Simple Pleasures

Kids' Little Treasure Books

   On Happy Families

   On What We've Learned . . . So Far

Life's Little Instructions from the Bible (with Rosemary C. Brown)

Life's Little Instruction Book™ *for Incurable Romantics* (with Robyn Spizman)

Lifes's Little Instruction Book™ *from Mothers to Daughters* (with Kim Shea)

A Book of Love for My Daughter (with Kim Shea and Paula Y. Flautt)

REMEMBRANCES

Compiled by Hy Brett

INTRODUCTION

My son, Steven, was a late walker, certainly later than his sister and cousins, but we took comfort in the periodic assurances of Dr. Stein, his pediatrician, that he would walk when the time was right for him. Weeks passed, and we thought the time would never come.

One brisk Sunday morning we put him into his stroller and took him out to Marine Park in Brooklyn. There, as far as the eye could see, the paths and fields were dense with geese. Suddenly Steven cried a single and unexpected word: "Out!" When we removed him from the stroller and took him by the hand, he began to walk faster and faster among the scattering birds. It was as if he had been walking for weeks. He was particularly attracted to a certain small goose with yellow specks, and as it flapped its wings and flew away, he even gave a leap after it. Then he looked up at us and laughed with delight at his accomplishment.

My wife and I always remembered that special day, particularly when we cheered Steven on at his baseball games at the same park. As Steven grew, we searched deliberately for ways to develop not only his body but also the moral and spiritual qualities that would lead to his personal fulfillment. We encouraged him to be aware of the dreams and ambitions that he was capable of realizing, and we read him poems and stories—some of which are included here—that offered him depictions of the world awaiting him, both its brightness and its shadows.

Our remembrances of our son are filled with joy; the dreams we shared with him have borne fruit, enabling him to become a blessing to family, friends, and strangers. Thanks to a lot of prayer and help from God, Steven turned out wonderfully, even though he never signed one of those multimillion-dollar contracts with the Yankees.

—Hy Brett

'Tis a happy thing
To be a father unto many sons.

—Shakespeare

Sons are the anchors of a mother's life.

—Sophocles

Call not that man wretched who, whatever ills he suffers, has a child to love.

—Robert Southey

As arrows are in the hand of a mighty man; so are children of the youth. Happy is the man that hath his quiver full of them.

—Psalms 127:4–5

A son is a stepping stone to immortality.

—Martin Chan

The potential possibilities of any child are the most intriguing and stimulating in all creation.

—Ray L. Wilbur

A son grows nine months in his mother's womb, and for all the rest of his life in the hearts of his parents.

—Eddie Costas

TO MY UNBORN SON

"My son!" What simple, beautiful words!
　"My boy!" What a wonderful phrase!
We're counting the months till you come to us—
　The months, and the weeks, and the days!

"The new little stranger," some babes are called,
　But that's not what you're going to be;
With double my Virtues and half of my faults,
　You can't be a stranger to me!

Your mother is straight as a sapling plant,
　The cleanest and best of her clan—
You're bone of her bone, and flesh of her flesh,
　And, by heaven, we'll make you a man!

Soon I shall take you in two strong arms—
    You that shall howl for joy—
With a simple, passionate, wonderful pride
    Because you are just my boy!

And you shall lie in your mother's arms,
    And croon at your mother's breast,
And I shall thank God I am there to shield
    The two that I love the best.

A wonderful thing is a breaking wave,
    And sweet is the scent of spring,
But the silent voice of an unborn babe
    Is God's most beautiful thing.

We're listening now to that silent voice
  And waiting, your mother and I—
Waiting to welcome the fruit of our love
  When you come to us by and by.

We're hungry to show you a wonderful world
  With wonderful things to be done,
We're aching to give you the best of us both
  And we're lonely for you—my son!

—Captain Cyril Morton Thorne

The childhood shows the man as morning shows the day.

—Milton

Of all wild beasts, a boy is the most difficult to manage.

—Plato

Whether king or peasant, he is happy who raises a virtuous son.

—F. L. Holland

The only thing that brings a mother undiluted satisfaction is her relation to a son. It is quite the almost complete relationship between human beings, and the one that is the most free from ambivalence.

—Sigmund Freud

Your son at five is your master, at ten your slave, at fifteen your double, and after that, your friend or your foe, depending on his bringing up.

—Hasdai Ibn Shaprut

He who rears his son to be righteous will be like an immortal.

—Rashi

My babe so beautiful! It thrills my heart
With tender gladness, thus to look at thee,
And think that thou shalt learn far other lore,
And in far other scenes!

—Samuel Taylor Coleridge

Children are our most valuable natural resource.

—Herbert Hoover

Do miracles still happen? Ask the parents of a newborn.

—Dianna Booher

Each child carries his own blessings into the world.

—Jewish Proverb

Heaven lies about us in our infancy!

—William Wordsworth

One chestnut, only one
Is all his tiny hands can hold,
My little baby son.

—Gomei

Children are poor men's riches.

—Universal Proverb

BIRTHDAY VERSES

Good morrow to the golden morning,
Good morrow to the world's delight—
I've come to bless thy life's beginning,
Since it makes my own so bright.

—Thomas Hood

Babies are such a nice way to start people.

—Don Herold

The family is one of nature's masterpieces.

—George Santayana

MOZART REPORTS ON THE BIRTH OF HIS SON

My Very Dear Father,

   Thank God, my wife has now survived the two critical days—yesterday and the day before, and in the circumstances is very well. We now hope all will go well. The child too is quite strong and healthy and has a tremendous number of things to do, I mean, drinking, sleeping, yelling . . . dribbling and so forth. He kisses the hands of his grandpa and of his aunt.

A happy family is but an earlier heaven.

—Sir John Bowring

Who can foretell for what high cause
This darling of the gods was born?

—Andrew Marvell

How many hopes and fears, how many ardent wishes and anxious apprehensions are twisted together in the threads that connect the parent with the child!

—Samuel G. Goodrich

At the age of four, I saw my father pour ketchup into the chicken soup that my mother had spent hours to prepare. After that, nothing can surprise me about family life.

—Melvin Klein

Yet the notion that a child is a guest in the house, to be loved and respected, but never possessed, is a truth as old as the sacred scripts of the Vedanta.

—Helge Rubinstein

One of my favorite childhood memories is greeting my father as he came home from work.

My mother, who worked an evening shift at the hospital, would leave the house around three in the afternoon. Dad would arrive home at three-thirty. My brother and I were left alone for that half-hour with strict instructions not to leave the house until Dad arrived.

We would take our positions on the couch and watch cartoons, always keeping one ear alert to the driveway. Even the best "Daffy Duck" would be abandoned when we heard his car.

I can remember running out to meet Dad and getting swept up in his big (often sweaty) arms. As he carried me toward the house, he'd put his big-brimmed straw hat on my head, and for a moment I'd be a cowboy. We'd sit on the porch as he removed his oily work boots (never allowed in the house). As he took them off I'd pull them on, and for a moment I'd be a wrangler. Then we'd go indoors and open his lunch pail. Any leftover snacks, which he always seemed to have, were for my brother and me to split.

It was great. Boots, hats, and snacks. What more could a five-year-old want?

—Max Lucado

Behold the child, by nature's kindly law
Pleased with a rattle, tickled with a straw.

—Alexander Pope

A child is fed with milk and praise.

—Mary Lamb

I love these little people; and it is not a slight thing when
they, who are so fresh from God, love us.

—Charles Dickens

SONG FOR THE NEWBORN

Newborn, we tenderly
In our arms take it,
Making good thoughts.
House-god, be entreated,
That it may grow from childhood to manhood,
Happy, contented;
Beautifully walking
The trail to old age.
Having good thoughts of the earth its mother,
That she may give it the fruits of her being.
Newborn, on the naked sand
Nakedly lay it.

—Pueblo song, translated by Mary Austin

Of all the joys that brighten suffering earth,
What joy is welcomed like a newborn child?

—Caroline Norton

Every man is an impossibility until he is born.

—Ralph Waldo Emerson

At twenty a man is full of fight and hope. He wants to reform the world. When he is seventy he still wants to reform the world, but he knows he can't.

—Clarence Darrow

MIGHTY LIKE A ROSE

Sweetest little feller—
Everybody knows;
Don't know what to call 'im,
But he's mighty like a rose;
Lookin' at his mammy with eyes so shiny blue
Makes you think that Heaven is comin' close to you.

—Frank L. Stanton

It is a wise child that knows his own father.

—Homer

It is a wise father that knows his own child.

—Shakespeare

You have to love your children unselfishly. That is hard. But it is the only way.

—Barbara Bush

Before I got married, I had six theories about bringing up children. Now I have six children and no theories.

—John Wilmot

There is no finer investment for any community than putting milk into babies.

—Winston Churchill

Our son, Martin, had a bad cold that morning, and for the first time in memory he couldn't accompany me to Mrs. Jefferson's village store to buy the Sunday paper and to have our Sunday breakfast treat of her homemade muffins and biscuits. I could never be sure whether the outing was more of a treat for Martin or for me.

Mrs. Jeffers stared at me a moment as I walked over to the counter with the newspaper, and then she said, "Is that you, Mr. Hansen?"

"It's me," I assured her.

She shook her head. "I didn't recognize you at first."

"How come?"

"Your boy's not with you this morning."

"It's still me," I told her, "but I certainly feel very different without him. I don't feel like myself at all."

—Arnold Hansen

Rest in soft peace, and, ask'd, say here doth lye
Ben. Jonson his best piece of poetrie.

—Ben Jonson, lines written on the
death of his first son

The soul is healed by being with children.

—Fyodor Dostoevsky

Children are the keys of paradise.

—Richard Henry Stoddard

They are the sons and daughters of Life's

longing for itself . . .

You may house their bodies but not their souls,

or their souls dwell in the house of tomorrow,

which you cannot visit, not even in your dreams.

—Kahlil Gilbran

Many children, many cares; no children, no felicity.

—Christian Nevell Bovee

We can't form our children on our own concepts; we must take them and love them as God gives them to us.

—Goethe

The easiest way to convince my kids they don't need anything is to get it for them.

—Joan Collins

Oh! the old swimming hole! When I last saw the place,
The scene was all changed, like the change in my face.

—James Whitcomb Riley

We find delight in the beauty and happiness of children that
makes the heart too big for the body.

—Ralph Waldo Emerson

The potential possibilities of any child are the most intriguing and stimulating in all creation.

—Ray L. Wilbur

Children are curious and are risk takers. They have lots of courage. They venture out into a world that is immense and dangerous. A child initially trusts life and the processes of life.

—John Bradshaw

He that raises a large family does, indeed, while he lives to observe them, stand a broader mark for sorrow; but then he stands a broader mark for pleasure too.

—Benjamin Franklin

The family is the school of duties . . . founded on love.

—Felix Adler

Our home joys are the most delightful life affords, and the joy of parents in their children is the most holy joy of humanity. It makes their hearts pure and good, it lifts men up to their Father in heaven.

—Johann Pestalozzi

They are idols of hearts and of households;
They are angels of God in disguise;
His sunlight still sleeps in their tresses;
His glory still gleams in their eyes.
Oh, those truants from home and from heaven,
They have made me more manly and mild,
And I know now how Jesus could liken
The kingdom of God to a child.

—Charles Dickens

This is a birthday letter to wish you many happy returns of the day. I wish we could have been together, but we shall meet again soon and then we will have treats. I have sent you two picture books, one about Br'er Rabbit, from Daddy, and one about other animals, from Mummy. And we have sent you a boat, painted red, with mast and sails to sail in the round pond by the windmill— and Mummy has sent you a boat hook to catch it when it comes ashore. Also, Mummy has sent you some sand toys to play in the sand with, and a card game.

—Kenneth Grahame, to his son Alastair

Where children are, there is the golden age.

—Novalis

Of all the joys that lighten suffering earth, what joy is welcomed like a newborn child?

—Caroline Norton

A babe in the house is a wellspring of pleasure, a messenger of peace and love, a resting place for innocence on earth, a link between angels and men.

— Martin F. Tupper

INSCRIPTION FOR MY LITTLE SON'S SILVER PLATE

When thou dost eat from off this plate,
I charge thee be thou temperate;
Unto thine elders at the board
Do thou sweet reverence accord;
And, though to dignity inclined,
Unto the serving-folk be kind;
Be ever mindful of the poor,
Nor turn them hungry from the door;
And unto God, for health and food
And all that in thy life is good,
Give thou thy heart in gratitude.

— Eugene Field

Never despair of a boy. The one you weep the most for at the mercy-seat may fill your heart with the sweetest joys.

—T. L. Cuyler

A boy's will is the wind's will,
And the thoughts of youth are long, long thoughts.

—Henry Wadsworth Longfellow

If thou would be a wise man, beget a son for the pleasing of God.

—Ptah-Hotep

A house is never perfectly furnished for enjoyment unless there is a child and a kitten in it.

—Robert Southey

What are little boys made of?
Snips and snails and puppy dogs' tails;
That's what little boys are made of.

—Anonymous

Like all children, I began to speculate on the problems of existence at an early age. I remember thinking of myself afloat—like a balloonist—in the atmosphere of life. I had come there I knew not how, but I knew I had got to come down sooner or later, and the thought was not welcome.

—Oliver Wendell Holmes

You know children are growing up when they start asking questions that have answers.

—John Plomp

What a difference it makes to come home to a child!

—Margaret Fuller

Nothing brings a man face-to-face with his responsibilities—and his blessings—more than the touch of his son's small hand slipping into his own.

—David Charles

Ah! happy years! once more who would not be a boy?

—Lord Byron

The scenes of childhood are the memories of future years.

—J. O. Choules

When the first baby laughed for the first time, the laugh broke into a million pieces, and they all went skipping about. That was the beginning of fairies.

—James M. Barrie

A boy is an appetite with a skin pulled over it.

—Anonymous

THE BABY

Where did you come from baby dear?
Out of the everywhere into here.
Where did you get those eyes so blue?
Out of the sky as I came through.
What makes the light in them sparkle and spin?
Some of the starry spikes left in.
Where did you get that little tear?
I found it waiting when I got here.
What makes your forehead so smooth and high?
A soft hand stroked it as I went by.
What makes your cheek like a warm white rose?
I saw something better than anyone knows.
Whence that three-cornered smile of bliss?

Three angels gave me at once a kiss.
Where did you get this pearly ear?
God spoke, and it came out to hear.
Where did you get those arms and hands?
Love made itself into bonds and bands.
Feet, whence did you come, you darling things?
From the same box as the cherub's wings.
How did they all just come to be you?
God thought about me, and so I grew.
But how did you come to us, you dear?
God thought about you, and so I am here.

—George Macdonald

The house came alive with the sound of slamming doors. Books skidded across the table, coming to rest precariously close to the edge. My eleven-year-old son was home from school. I started to hug him, but resisted the urge. Motherly gestures had become unpopular lately.

"Hey, Mom! Guess what! Mr. Travers, our gym instructor, has arranged a camp-out at Bear Lake. Can I go?"

"Slow down," I said, my stomach muscles stiffening. "Bear Lake is a long way from here."

"It won't cost a lot, Mom," he continued, ignoring my apprehension. "I'll need a pup tent, but there's my newspaper route. And I could mow lawns."

My mind scrambled for excuses. "I'll think about it," I said.

"I have to know by Friday." His voice was low.

I had three days to consider. Four nights to lie awake and worry. How could I let him go? What if something happened to him?

On Wednesday, Greg and I worked on his school project, a complicated series of switches and buttons and a bell. I had tried to talk him into something simpler, but that was what he wanted to do.

I reached out to hold a wire for him. His fingers were deft as they tightened the nut. And suddenly I noticed that his hands were bigger than mine. I closed my eyes and saw baby fingers struggling with shoelaces. When had Greg's hands become so square and steady and large?

I took a deep breath and touched Greg's shoulder. "I've been wondering." My voice was steady. The fear was gone, though I knew it would come back. I'd have to grapple with it again and again. "Is it too early in the season to shop for a pup tent?"

Understanding burst across his face. "Oh, Mom. Thank you!"

He flung himself at me in a big bear hug. I held him close for just a moment, but lightly this time, ready to let go.

—Margaret Chittenden (adapted)

Every child walks into existence through the golden gate of love.

—Henry Ward Beecher

What gift has Providence bestowed on man that is so dear to him as his children?

—Plutarch

I seem, for my own part, to see the benevolence of the Deity more clearly in the pleasures of young children than in anything else in the world.

—William Paley

Oh, would I were a boy again,
When life seemed formed of sunny years
And all the heart then knew of pain
Was wept away in transient tears.

—Mark Lemon

A walk in the woods with my little boy is a walk in a world filled with wonder.

—Jack Phillips

The parent is low, who having children, truly feels bored.

—Jean Paul

Parents are not quite interested in justice, they are interested in quiet.

—Bill Cosby

WORK IN PROGRESS

Sticky hands and dirty faces,
Scuffed-up shoes with untied laces;
Baseball cards and cookie crumbs,
Secret projects made "all thumbs";
Pockets filled with untold treasure,
Hearts with love beyond all measure—
Who are these strange, mysterious ones?
The precious creatures moms call sons.

—Barbara Brett

The charm, one might say the genius of memory, is that it is choosy, chancy, and temperamental: it rejects the edifying cathedral and indelibly photographs the small boy outside, chewing a hunk of melon in the dust.

—Elizabeth Bowen

Who can measure the magic of the treasures to be found in the pockets of her son's overalls at the end of the day?

—Jennifer Coles

I took a good deal o' pains with his eddication, sir; let him run in the streets when he was very young, and shift for hisself. It's the only way to make a boy sharp, sir.

—Charles Dickens

There are perhaps no days of our childhood we lived so fully as those we spent with a favorite book.

—Marcel Proust

Give a little love to a child, and you get a great deal back.

—John Ruskin

Children have but little idea how the hearts of their parents yearn over them. When they grow up and have children of their own, then they understand and sigh, and sigh when it is too late. If you live to be old you will never forget how your father and mother came to visit you at Harvard and tried so hard to do something for you. When I was your age and was at school at Ashland, father and mother came one afternoon in a sleigh and spent a couple of hours with me. They brought me some mince pies and apples. The plain old farmer and his plain old wife, how awkward and curious they looked amid the throng of young people, but how precious the thought and memory of them is to me.

—John Burroughs, to his son Julian

Parents can plant magic in a child's mind through certain words spoken with some thrilling quality of voice, some uplift of the heart and spirit.

—Robert Macneil

Do not train boys to learning by force and harshness, but lead them by what amuses them, so that they may better discover the bent of their minds.

—Plato

Ah! what would the world be to us,
If the children were no more?
We should dread the desert behind us
Worse than the dark before.

—Henry Wadsworth Longfellow

Behold one of the greatest pleasures of childhood is found
in the mysteries it hides from the skepticism of the elders,
and works up into small mythologies of its own.

—Oliver Wendell Holmes

Our notion of the perfect society embraces the family as
its center and ornament. Nor is there a paradise planted till
the children appear in the foreground to animate and complete the picture.

—Amos Bronson Alcott

Child, you are like a flower,
So sweet and pure and fair.
I look at you, and sadness
Touches me with a prayer.

—Heinrich Heine

Craig Cabaniss, senior pastor of Grace Church in San Diego, came upon his toddler son joyfully singing the word "Alleluia" as he ascended the stairs of their home. As the little boy climbed, his volume increased and the chorus he sang gained momentum. Craig was impressed with his son's ability to vary his note selection. Immediately Craig's mind began to fill with the potential of this newly demonstrated skill. Perhaps his boy would lead worship for assembled thousands; maybe he'd write praise songs that would one day be considered classics; who knows, the boy might even land a recording contract.

Craig was suddenly cast back to reality when his son reached the top stair and built up to a crescendo for his grand finale. His tiny lungs filled with air and then his voice belted out, "Alleluia . . . tooooo . . . meeeee!"

—Michael W. Smith (adapted)

How dear to my heart are the scenes of my childhood,
When fond recollection presents them to view:
The orchard, the meadow, the deep-tangled wildwood,
And every lov'd spot which my infancy knew.

—William Wordsworth

My mother loved children—she would have given anything if I had been one.

—Groucho Marx

In every dispute between parent and child, both cannot be right, but they may be, and usually are, both wrong. It is this situation which gives family life its peculiar hysterical charm.

—Isaac Rosenfeld

Grown men can learn from very little children, for the hearts of little children are pure.

Therefore, the Great Spirit may show to them many things which older people miss.

—Black Elk

MY SON NEEDS A FATHER

I am a widow with a boy of three. His name is Teddy. I've met a man, Al, who will make him a great father, but he is allergic to my three cats. They are spayed, house trained, love children, and are not fussy eaters. If you would like to adopt one or more of my cats, please inquire inside for more information. Thank you and God bless.

—Sign in a Laundromat on Kings Highway in Brooklyn

There is always one moment in childhood when the door opens and lets the future in.

—Graham Greene

I couldn't love my son more if he were painted by Norman Rockwell.

—Thomas Weede

Behold, children are a heritage from the Lord, the fruit of the womb is a reward.

—Psalms 127: 3

One of the greatest joys in life is watching your son hit the homer that wins the game for his team. One of the greatest responsibilities in life is showing him that you still love him and that life goes on and will even get better when he misses that same fateful pitch.

—John Wilkens

OVER THE HILLS AND FAR AWAY

Over the hills and far away,
A little boy steals from his morning play,
And under the blossoming apple-tree
He lies and dreams of the things to be:
Of battles fought and of victories won,
Of wrongs o'erthrown and of great deeds done—
Of the valor that he shall prove some day,
Over the hills and far away—
Over the hills and far away!

—— Eugene Field

That unfeathered two-legged thing, a son.

—John Dryden

A boy has two jobs. One is just being a boy. The other is growing up to be a man.

—Herbert Hoover

If children grew up according to early indications, we should have nothing but geniuses.

—Goethe

Ah, then how sweetly closed those crowded days!
The minutes parting one by one like rays,
   That fade upon a summer's eve.
But O, what charm or magic numbers
Can give me back the gentle slumbers
   Those weary, happy days did leave?
When by my bed I saw my mother kneel,
   And with her blessing took her nightly kiss;
   Whatever Time destroys, he cannot this;—
E'en now that nameless kiss I feel.

—Washington Allston

There was never a child so lovely but his mother was glad to get him to sleep.

—Ralph Waldo Emerson

The genuine human boy may, I think, be set down as the noblest work of God.

—Charles B. Fairbanks

We worry about what a child will be tomorrow, yet we forget that he is someone today.

—Stacia Tauscher

The stories of childhood leave an indelible impression, and their author always has a niche in the temple of memory from which the image is never cast out to be thrown on the rubbish heap of things that are outgrown and outlived.

—Howard Pyle

Perhaps a child who is fussed over gets a feeling of destiny; he thinks he is in the world for something important and it gives him drive and confidence.

—Dr. Benjamin Spock

I was very glad to receive your little letter. Mind that you and Lionel do not quarrel and vex poor mama who has lots of work to do, and learn your lessons regularly, for gentlemen and ladies will not take you for a gentleman when you grow up if you are ignorant.

—Alfred Lord Tennyson, to his son Hallam

The father is always a Republican toward his son, and his mother's always a Democrat.

—Robert Frost

For rarely are sons similar to their fathers: most are worse, and a few are better than their fathers.

—Homer

His father watched him across the gulf of years and pathos which always must divide a father from his son.

—John Marquand

One a penny, two a penny, hot cross buns;
If you have no daughters, give them to your sons.

—Anonymous

The smallest children are nearest to God, as the smallest
planets are nearest the sun.

—Jean Paul Richter

Each child is an adventure into a better life—an opportunity to change the old pattern and make it new.

—Hubert H. Humphrey

THE BOY

Go, little boy,
Fill thee with joy;
For Time gives thee
Unlicensed hours,
To run in fields,
And roll in flowers.
A little boy
Can life enjoy;
If but to see
The horses pass,
When shut indoors
Behind the glass.

Go, little boy,
Fill thee with joy;
Fear not, like man,
The kick of wrath,
That you do lie
In some one's path.
Time is to thee
Eternity,
As to a bird
Or butterfly;
And in that faith
True joy doth lie.

—W. H. Davis

When you can't do anything else to a boy, you can make him wash his face.

—Ed Howe

I have always attributed my son's passion for sushi to the fact that he took his first steps during a Japanese spring festival at the botanical garden. I thank God daily that he never became a sumo wrestler.

—Mel Abrams

When Mother reads aloud, I long
For noble deeds to do—
To help the right, redress the wrong;
It seems so easy to be strong,
So simple to be true.
Oh, thick and fast the visions crowd
My eyes, when Mother reads aloud.

—Anonymous

A child is a curly, dimpled lunatic.

—Ralph Waldo Emerson

Little children are still the symbol of the eternal marriage between love and duty.

—George Eliot

A dining room table with children's eager, hungry faces around it ceases to be merely a dining room table, and becomes an altar.

—Simeon Strunsky

Parents lend children their experience and a vicarious memory; children endow their parents with a vicarious immortality.

—George Santayana

When I was a boy of fourteen, my father was so ignorant I could hardly stand to have the old man around. But when I got to be twenty-one, I was astonished at how much the old man had learned in seven years.

—Mark Twain

ELEGY FOR MY SON

Dear Lord, receive my son, whose winning love
To me was like a friendship, far above
The course of nature, or his tender age,
Whose looks could all my bitter griefs assuage.
Let his pure soul, ordained seven years to be,
In that frail body, which was part of me,
Remain my pledge in heaven, as sent to show
How to this port at every step I go.

—John Beaumont

Family jokes, though rightly cursed by strangers, are the bond that keeps most families alive.

—Stella Benson

Fatherhood is pretending the present you love most is soap-on-a-rope.

—Bill Cosby

Let a man turn to his own childhood—no further—if he will renew his sense of remoteness, and of the mystery of change.

—Alice Meynell

Every child born into the world is a new thought of God,
an ever-fresh and radiant possibility.

—Kate Douglas Wiggin

Those lives are, indeed, narrow and confined which are not
blessed with several children.

—John Burroughs

Children are unpredictable. You never know what inconsis-
tency they're going to catch you in next.

—Franklin P. Jones

There is something about the relationship [between fathers and sons] that is pretty difficult to put your finger on. I think fathers realize this and have it on their minds a good deal more than their sons realize.

—Sherwood Anderson

Would God I had died for thee, O Absalom, my son, my son!

—2 Samuel 18:33

It isn't easy in a world filled with violence to teach children that they should never resort to force to settle their differences, but I tried. I was sure I had failed the day my eight-year-old came home with a whopping big shiner.

"What have I told you about fighting?" I asked, applying a compress.

"But, Mom, I wasn't fighting," he protested. "I was breaking up a fight. This kid from fifth grade was picking on my friend."

"And did you succeed?" I asked.

He gave me a slow, proud smile. "Yeah. He ran away."

I smiled back and hugged him, confident that I had succeeded too.

—Natalie Brooks

It is dangerous to confuse children with angels.

—David Fyfe

I am convinced that every boy, in his heart, would rather steal second base than an automobile.

—Thomas Campbell Clark

The distinction between children and adults, while probably useful for some purposes, is at bottom a specious one, I feel. There are only individual egos, crazy for love.

—Don Barthelme

THE BAREFOOT BOY

Blessings on thee, little man,
Barefoot boy with cheeks of tan . . .
From my heart I give thee joy—
I was once a barefoot boy! . . .
Oh! for boyhood's painless play,
Sleep that wakes in laughing day,
Health that mocks the doctor's rule,
Knowledge never learned of schools . . .
Oh, for boyhood's time of June
Crowding years in one brief moon,
When all things I heard or saw,
Me, their master, waited for.

—John Greenleaf Whittier

The best way to look back at childhood is with rose-colored glasses.

—George Burns

My father was a strict disciplinarian. He never permitted me to read the Sunday comics until he was through with them himself.

—Bert Henry

Youth comes but once in a lifetime.

—Henry Wadsworth Longfellow

One more year of loving you; one less year to love you in. That is the sad side. Meanwhile, without totting up the time that remains, let us love each other as much as we can.

—Alexander Dumas, New Year's greeting
to his son Alexander, Jr.

My mother had a great deal of trouble with me, but I think she enjoyed it.

—Mark Twain

The fact that boys are allowed to exist at all is evidence of a remarkable Christian forbearance among men.

—Ambrose Bierce

Dealing with daughters does not prepare parents for dealing with a son.

—Horace Wilcox

A BOY

Out of the noise of tired people working,
    Harried with thoughts of war and lists of dead,
His beauty met me like a fresh wind blowing,
    Clean boyish beauty and high-held head.
Eyes that told secrets, lips that would not tell them,
Fearless and shy the young unwearied eyes—
Men die by millions now, because God blunders,
    Yet to have made this boy he must be wise.

—Sara Teasdale

The glory of the nation rests in the character of her men. And character comes from boyhood. Thus every boy is a challenge to his elders.

—Herbert Hoover

The survivorship of a worthy man in his son is a pleasure scarce inferior to the hopes of the continuance of his own life.

—Richard Steele

What gift has Providence bestowed on man that is so dear to him as his children?

—Cicero

A man can never quite understand a boy, even when he has been a boy.

—Gilbert K. Chesterton

The only time a woman really succeeds in changing a man is when he's a baby.

—Natalie Wood

Indisputedly, a great, good, handsome man is the first of created things.

—Charlotte Brontë

There's no greater embarrassment to a father than a son who can't hit the spittoon at less than eight feet.

—Dutch Cooley

The father who does not teach his son his duties is equally guilty as the son who neglects them.

—Confucius

On a snowy day long before he became general of the Confederate army during the Civil War, Robert E. Lee took his son Custis, eight, out for a walk. The drifts were high, and Custis began to fall behind his father. Looking back, General Lee observed that the boy was imitating his movements and walking in his tracks. "When I saw this," Lee later told a friend, "I said to myself, 'It behooves me to walk very straight when this fellow is already following in my footsteps.'"

—Todd Duncan (adapted)

Age seventeen is the point in the journey when the parents retire to the observation car; it is the time when you stop being critical of your eldest son and he starts being critical of you.

—Sally and James Reston

Few men are clever enough to have the last word with a teenage son.

—Hy Brett

Youth is wholly experimental.

—Robert Louis Stevenson

He capers, he dances, he has eyes of youth, he writes verses, he speaks holiday, he smells April and May.

—Shakespeare

Children need love, especially when they don't deserve it.

—Harold Hulbert

When I hand my son the keys to the car I always remind him that his mother's heart is hanging unseen on the ring.

—Nat Service

A father complained to the Baalshem [head rabbi] that his son had forsaken God.

"What, Rabbi, shall I do?"

"Love him more than ever," the Baalshem instructed.

—Hasidic story

A wise parent humors the desire for independent action, so as to become the friend and advisor when his absolute rule shall cease.

—Elizabeth Gaskell

He that will have his son have a respect for him and his orders, must himself have a great reverence for his son.

—John Locke

It is impossible to please all the world and one's father.

—Jean de La Fontaine

I have found that the best way to give advice to your children is to find out what they want and then advise them to do it.

—Harry Truman

No more of this [attempted suicide]! Only come to my arms, you shall not hear one harsh word. For God's sake do not rush to destruction. You shall be received with as much affection as ever. As to what is to be thought of and done for the future, we will talk it over in a friendly way together. Upon my word of honor, you shall hear no reproaches, which indeed can now do no good. You have nothing to expect from me but the most anxious and loving care and help. Only come, come to the heart of your father. Come at once on receipt of this!

—Ludwig van Beethoven, to his adopted son Karl

Blessed be the hand that prepares a pleasure for a child, for there is no saying when and where it may bloom forth.

—Douglas Jerrold

No matter how old a son gets, he never forgets the bar mitzvah presents from his parents.

—Jewish saying

For many children, joy comes as the result of mining something unique and wondrous about themselves from some inner shaft.

—Thomas J. Cottle

There are three ways to get something done: do it yourself, employ someone, or forbid your children to do it.

—Monta Crane

Only a mother's heart can be
Patient enough for such as he.

—Ethel Lynn Beers

One of the most obvious facts about grownups to a child is that they have forgotten what it is like to be a child.

—Randall Jarrell

THE RETURN

He went, and he was gay to go;
And I smiled on him as he went.
My son, 'twas well he couldn't know
My darkest dread, nor what it meant—
Just what it meant to smile and smile
And let my son go cheerily—
My son . . . and wondering all the while
What stranger would come back to me.

—Wilfred Gibson

One word frees us of all the weight and pain of life. That word is love.

—Sophocles

There is no greater demonstration of the power of heredity than a father and son who laugh at the same nutty jokes.

—Ruth Shelling

A boy is a magical creature—you can lock him out of your workshop, but you can't lock him out of your heart.

—Allan Beck

Don't laugh at a youth for his imperfections; he is only trying on one face after another to find a face of his own.

—Logan Pearsall Smith

A son who can eat a whole pepperoni pizza at two in the morning is destined to lead an interesting life.

—Fran Mancuso

We had good luck with our sons. They grew up before we knew it.

—Mamie Tucker

A wise son maketh a glad father: but a foolish son is the heaviness of his mother.

—Proverbs 10:1

Children are God's apostles, sent forth, day by day, to preach of love and hope and peace.

—James Russell Lowell

As long as the language contains the words "What's for dinner?" a mother never has to worry about keeping the lines of communication open with her teenage son.

—Henrietta Messier

There are times when parenthood seems nothing more than feeding the hand that bites you.

—Peter De Vries

Adults are obsolete children.

—Dr. Seuss

Like most children, my son had been eager for the day when he would be a "big boy" and go to school, and when the day finally came for him to enter kindergarten, he was ecstatic. He came home that first day still full of enthusiasm. But as the week wore on, he became quieter and quieter.

"What's the matter?" I asked. "Don't you like school?"

He looked up at me, his face stricken. "Oh, Mommy, kindergarten is so hard!"

My heart sank. My son was a child who was filled with curiosity. He'd always loved being read to and playing school. "Don't you like story time and learning new things?" I prodded.

His eyes lit up. "I love story time and learning things! Today the teacher taught us science. That's really fun. We're going to grow grass on a sponge!"

"Then, if you love learning, why are you so sad?"

"The learning's fun—it's the rest of the work that's so hard!" He sighed like an old man with the burdens of the world on his shoulders. "All that cutting and pasting and coloring!"

***

My son is grown-up now. He's a molecular biologist and a professor at a prestigious university. Every time he takes me on a tour of his laboratory, filled with enthusiasm as he tells me about his work, I'm reminded of that day and I have to smile. All his life, learning has remained fun—a true labor of love. As for the cutting and pasting and coloring—well, he can draw a mean diagram when he has to!

—Maxine Greenstein

A boy becomes an adult three years before his parents think he does, and about two years after he thinks he does.

—Lewis B. Hershey

The best way to make children good is to make them happy.

—Oscar Wilde

Perhaps host and guest is really the happiest relation for father and son.

—Evelyn Waugh

There's at least one good thing about a son. He spends less time in the bathroom than a wife or daughter.

—Barry Ames

I would give everything to my son except the keys to my humidor.

—Winston Churchill

The best thing a father can do for a son is to give him forty pounds and throw him out the door.

—W. Somerset Maugham

Youth's the season made for joys,
Love is then our duty.

—John Gay

The sweetest roamer is a young boy's heart.

—George E. Woodberry

I was never more pleased with my son than on the day he
saw a John Wayne western on TV and told me I could have
handled those rustlers just as well.

—Evan McNaughton

My wife is always comparing our daughter Susan to a flower—sometimes a rose, sometimes a daisy. But I've never been able to think of a single flower that I can compare our son Henry to. Frankly, I'm kind of glad about that.

—Warren Fitch

My son is twenty-two, and the most memorable gift I ever received from him is the case of measles he brought home from school.

—Frank Scholle

I am the family face;
Flesh perishes, I live on,
Projecting trait and trace
Through time to times anon,
And leaping from, place to place
Over oblivion.

—Thomas Hardy

There comes a day when you know in your heart that your son is going to come out right. In my family, it was when our boy Tom did not try to sell his school's fund-raising cookies to a neighbor who was on a reducing diet.

—Loretta Stores

He who is survived by a son devoted to Torah is as though he had not died.

—Simeon ben Yohai

In the man whose childhood has known caresses, there is always a fiber of memory that can be touched to gentler issues.

—George Eliot

For a son to think harshly of his parents profits only his therapist.

—Eddie Marris

One of my early memories is of my folks taking me to the Central Park Zoo in New York City. It was at the height of the Great Depression, and my dad had lost his job. He offered me a choice of a pony ride or a balloon. I chose the balloon. Over the years, I told myself that someday I would come back to the zoo with my own son and he would have both the ride and the balloon.

Eventually, my dream came true. As I watched Bobby with his balloon in the pony cart, I felt richer than the millionaires who lived across Fifth Avenue in their penthouses. Also, I knew that my own dad was with us in spirit, and that his prayers had contributed to this happy day.

—Robert Erskine

A man isn't poor if he has a rich son.

—Hy Brett

It takes a woman twenty years to make a man of her son, and another woman twenty minutes to make a fool of him.

—Helen Rowland

Our children are not going to be just "our children"—they are going to be other people's husbands and wives and the parents of our grandchildren.

—Dr. Mary Calderone

You are told a lot about your education, but some beautiful, sacred memory, preserved since childhood, is perhaps the best education of all. If a man carries many such memories into life with him, he is saved for the rest of his days. And even if only one good memory is left in our hearts, it may also be the instrument of our salvation one day.

—Fyodor Dostoevski

A man travels the world over in search of what he needs and returns home to find it.

—George Moore

He followed in his father's footsteps, but his gait was somewhat erratic.

—Nicolas Bentley

A child becomes an adult when he realizes that he has a right not only to be right but also to be wrong.

—Thomas Szasz

You gotta be a man to play baseball for a living but you gotta have a lot of little boy in you too.

—Roy Campanella

Some sons grow up to be a chip off the old block. Mine became more of a splinter.

—Samuel Cleavon

Marry your son when you will, your daughter when you can.

—George Herbert

In Ernest Hemingway's short story "The Capitol of the World," a father and his teenage son suffer a breakdown in their relationship and the son runs away from home. The father undertakes a long but unsuccessful journey in search of his son. In desperation, the father places an advertisement in a Madrid newspaper: "Dear Paco, meet me in front of the newspaper office tomorrow at noon . . . all is forgiven . . . I love you." The next morning eight hundred men named Paco are waiting in front of the newspaper office, hoping to be reunited with their fathers.

With my luck, if I ever went to the trouble of fattening a calf for my prodigal son, he would turn out to be a vegetarian.

—Hy Brett

For thousands of years, father and son have stretched wistful hands across the canyon of time, each eager to help the other to his side, but neither quite able to desert the loyalties of his contemporaries. The relationship is always changing and hence always fragile; nothing endures except the sense of difference.

—Alan Valentine

By the time a man realizes that maybe his father was right, he usually has a son who thinks he's wrong.

—Charles Wadworth

My parents and I have been a constant source of astonishment to one another.

—Oscar Wilde

A son's memory of an event is never the same as that of his parents.

—Aldous Huxley

A boy can learn a lot from a dog: obedience, loyalty, and the importance of turning around three times before lying down.

—Robert Benchley

The representative of the highest spiritual authority of the earth is glad, indeed boasts, of being the son of a humble but robust and honest laborer.

—Pope John XXIII

One of the great joys of going down memory lane with a grown-up son is that he never wants you to stop for hamburgers and rest rooms.

—Hy Brett

When I was a boy I used to do what my father wanted. Now I have to do what my boy wants. My problem is: When am I going to do what I want?

—Sam Levenson

He only half dies who leaves an image of himself in his sons.

—Carlo Goldoni

Boys are beyond the range of anybody's sure understanding, at least when they are between the ages of eighteen months and ninety years.

—James Thurber

When a father gives to his son, both laugh; when a son gives to his father, both cry.

—Jewish proverb

But wherever they go, and whatever happens to them on the way, in that enchanted place on the top of the Forest, a little boy and his Bear will always be playing.

—A. A. Milne, closing lines of
The House at Pooh Corner

INSTRUCTIONS

Compiled by H. Jackson Brown, Jr.

INTRODUCTION

Life's Little Instruction Book began as thirty handwritten pages of fatherly advice jotted down while sitting at our breakfast room table. It was a gift to my son, Adam, as he began a new life as a college freshman.

My parenting philosophy was not to pave the road for my son but to provide him a road map. That's how I hoped he would use these heart and mind reflections.

Well, somehow those notes became a popular book and over the years two more volumes were added to the collection. I've selected my favorite 232 entries from these books for this publication. Adam tells me he still picks up the little plaid books from time to time and almost always discovers something that cheers and inspires him.

It is my hope that you, too, will find a few words here that help you smooth out some of life's wrinkles.

—H. Jackson Brown, Jr.

1 • Compliment three people every day.

2 • Have a dog.

3 • Watch a sunrise at least once a year.

4 • Remember other people's birthdays.

5 · Overtip breakfast waitresses.

6 · Use the good silver.

7 · Live beneath your means.

8 · Drive inexpensive cars, but own the best house you can afford.

9 · Be forgiving of yourself and others.

10 · Learn three clean jokes.

11 · Wear polished shoes.

12 · Floss your teeth.

13 · Drink champagne for no reason at all.

14 · Ask for a raise when you feel you've earned it.

15 · Never buy a house without a fireplace.

16 • Buy whatever kids are selling on card
   tables in their front yards.

17 • Once in your life own a convertible.

18 • Learn to identify the music of Chopin,
   Mozart, and Beethoven.

19 · Plant a tree on your birthday.

20 · Donate two pints of blood every year.

21 · Make new friends but cherish the old ones.

22 · Don't postpone joy.

23 · Write "thank you" notes promptly.

24 · Never give up on anybody. Miracles happen every day.

25 • Don't waste time learning the "tricks of the trade." Instead, learn the trade.

26 • Put the cap back on the toothpaste.

27 • Vote.

28 · Surprise loved ones with little unexpected gifts.

29 · Stop blaming others. Take responsibility for every area of your life.

30 · Never mention being on a diet.

31 · Live so that when your children think of fairness, caring, and integrity, they think of you.

32 · Admit your mistakes.

33 · Ask someone to pick up your mail and the daily paper when you're out of town. Those are the first two things potential burglars look for.

34 · Be brave. Even if you're not, pretend to be. No one can tell the difference.

35 · Whistle.

36 · Give to charity all the clothes you haven't worn during the past three years.

37 · Hug children after you discipline them.

38 · Don't take good health for granted.

39 · When someone wants to hire you, even if it's for a job you have little interest in, talk to them. Never close the door on an opportunity until you've had a chance to hear the offer in person.

40 · Don't mess with drugs, and don't associate with those who do.

41 · Forget the Joneses.

42 · Choose your life's mate carefully. From this one decision will come ninety percent of all your happiness or misery.

43 · Make it a habit to do nice things for people who'll never find out.

44 · Smile a lot. It costs nothing and is beyond price.

45 · Lend only those books you never care to see again.

46 · Know how to change a tire.

47 · Read the Bill of Rights.

48 · Attend class reunions.

49 · Never use profanity.

50 • Always have something beautiful in sight, even if it's just a daisy in a jelly glass.

51 • Give yourself a year and read the Bible cover to cover.

52 • Put a lot of little marshmallows in your hot chocolate.

53 · Stop and read historical roadside mark-ers.

54 · Learn to listen. Opportunity sometimes knocks very softly.

55 · Think big thoughts, but relish small pleasures.

56 · Know how to tie a bow tie.

57 · Leave the toilet seat in the down position.

58 · When someone is relating an important event that's happened to them, don't try to top them with a story of your own. Let them have the stage.

59 · Keep your watch five minutes fast.

60 · Learn Spanish. In a few years, more than thirty-five percent of all Americans will speak it as their first language.

61 · Never deprive someone of hope; it might be all they have.

62 · Let your representatives in Washington know how you feel. Call (202) 225-3121 for the House and (202) 224-3121 for the Senate. An operator will connect you to the right office.

63 · Turn off the television at dinner time.

64 · Sing in a choir.

65 · Get acquainted with a good lawyer, accountant, and plumber.

66 · Fly Old Glory on the Fourth of July.

67 · Resist the temptation to put a cute message on your answering machine.

68 · Pray not for things, but for wisdom and courage.

69 · Use seat belts.

70 · Have regular medical and dental check-ups.

71 · Don't waste time responding to your critics.

72 · Don't scrimp in order to leave money to your children.

73 · Never give up on what you really want to do. The person with big dreams is more powerful than one with all the facts.

74 · Be suspicious of all politicians.

75 · Be kinder than necessary.

76 · Encourage your children to have a part-
time job after the age of sixteen.

77 · Give people a second chance, but not a third.

78 · Read carefully anything that requires your signature. Remember the big print giveth and the small print taketh away.

79 · Learn to recognize the inconsequential, then ignore it.

80 · Be your wife's best friend.

81 · Do battle against prejudice and discrimination wherever you find them.

82 · Wear out, don't rust out.

83 · Be romantic.

84 · Be insatiably curious. Ask "why" a lot.

85 · Measure people by the size of their hearts, not the size of their bank accounts.

86 · Become the most positive and enthusiastic person you know.

87 · Don't worry that you can't give your kids the best of everything. Give them your very best.

88 · Don't forget, a person's greatest emotional need is to feel appreciated.

89 · Feed a stranger's expired parking meter.

90 · Park at the back of the lot at shopping centers. The walk is good exercise.

91 · Don't watch violent television shows, and don't buy products that sponsor them.

92 · Show respect for all living things.

93 · Swing for the fence.

94 · Observe the speed limit.

95 · Commit yourself to constant self-improvement.

96 · Take your dog to obedience school. You'll
   both learn a lot.

97 · Don't major in minor things.

98 · Don't plan a long evening on a blind date.
   A lunch date is perfect. If things don't
   work out, both of you have wasted only
   an hour.

99 · Don't discuss business in elevators. You never know who may overhear you.

100 · When complimented, a sincere "thank you" is the only response required.

101 · Think twice before burdening a friend with a secret.

102 · When someone hugs you, let them be the first to let go.

103 · Resist giving advice concerning matrimony, finances, or hairstyles.

104 · Teach your children the value of money and the importance of saving.

105 · Have impeccable manners.

106 · Never pay for work before it's completed.

107 · Keep good company.

108 · Keep a daily journal.

109 · Be willing to lose a battle in order to win the war.

110 · Watch the movie *It's a Wonderful Life* every Christmas.

111 · Drink eight glasses of water every day.

112 · Respect tradition.

113 · Be cautious about lending money to friends. You might lose both.

114 · Buy a bird feeder and hang it so that you can see it from your kitchen window.

115 · Never cut what can be untied.

116 · Wave at children on school buses.

117 · Show respect for others' time. Call
whenever you're going to be more than
ten minutes late for an appointment.

118 · Hire people smarter than you.

119 · Learn to show enthusiasm, even when you don't feel like it.

120 · Purchase gas from the neighborhood gas station even if it costs more. Next winter when it's six degrees and your car won't start, you'll be glad they know you.

121 • Don't jaywalk.

122 • Never ask a lawyer or accountant for business advice. They are trained to find problems, not solutions.

123 • Take family vacations whether you can afford them or not. The memories will be priceless.

124 · Beware of the person who has nothing to lose.

125 · Lie on your back and look at the stars.

126 · Don't leave car keys in the ignition.

127 · When facing a difficult task, act as though
it is impossible to fail. If you're going after
Moby Dick, take along the tartar sauce.

128 · Remember that overnight success usually
takes about fifteen years.

129 · Leave everything a little better than you
found it.

130 · Don't use a toothpick in public.

131 · Promise big. Deliver big.

132 · Don't delay acting on a good idea. Chances are someone else has just thought of it, too. Success comes to the one who acts first.

133 · Don't burn bridges. You'll be surprised how many times you have to cross the same river.

134 · Don't spread yourself too thin. Learn to say no politely and quickly.

135 · Accept pain and disappointment as part of life.

136 · Remember that a successful marriage depends on two things: (1) finding the right person and (2) being the right person.

137 · See problems as opportunities for growth and self-mastery.

138 · Don't expect life to be fair.

139 · Judge your success by the degree that you're enjoying peace, health, and love.

140 · Make the bed when you're an overnight visitor in someone's home.

141 · Refrain from envy. It's the source of much unhappiness.

142 · Remember the deal's not done until the check has cleared the bank.

143 · Be wary of people who tell you how honest they are.

144 · Remember that winners do what losers don't want to do.

145 · Install smoke detectors in your home.

146 · Live your life as an exclamation, not an explanation.

147 · Don't be fooled. If something sounds too good to be true, it probably is.

148 · Rekindle old friendships.

149 · Every so often, push your luck.

150 · Get your next pet from the animal shelter.

151 · Reread your favorite book.

152 ⋅ When renting a car for a couple of days, splurge and get the big Lincoln.

153 ⋅ Be bold and courageous. When you look back on your life, you'll regret the things you didn't do more than the ones you did.

154 ⋅ Never waste an opportunity to tell someone you love them.

155 · To explain a romantic break-up, simply say, "It was all my fault."

156 · When playing games with children, let them win.

157 · Be decisive even if it means you'll sometimes be wrong.

158 · Don't let anyone talk you out of pursuing what you know to be a great idea.

159 · Take charge of your attitude. Don't let someone else choose it for you.

160 · Acquire things the old-fashioned way: Save for them and pay cash.

161 · Remember no one makes it alone. Have a grateful heart and be quick to acknowledge those who help you.

162 · Be prepared to lose once in a while.

163 · Forget committees. New, noble, world-changing ideas always come from one person working alone.

164 · Pay attention to the details.

165 · Understand that happiness is not based on possessions, power, or prestige, but on relationships with people you love and respect.

166 · Never give a loved one a gift that suggests they need improvement.

167 · Wear expensive shoes, belts, and ties, but buy them on sale.

168 · Carry stamps in your wallet. You never know when you'll discover the perfect card for a friend or loved one.

169 · Never give anyone a fruitcake.

170 · Focus on making things better, not bigger.

171 · Don't be intimidated by doctors and nurses. Even when you're in the hospital, it's still your body.

172 · Don't flaunt your success, but don't apologize for it either.

173 · Every once in a while, take the scenic route.

174 · Don't let your possessions possess you.

175 · Wage war against littering.

176 · Cut your own firewood.

177 · Be enthusiastic about the success of others.

178 · Don't procrastinate. Do what needs doing when it needs to be done.

179 · Get your priorities straight. No one ever said on his deathbed, "Gee, if I'd only spent more time at the office."

180 · Take care of your reputation. It's your most valuable asset.

181 · Turn on your headlights when it begins to rain.

182 · Don't tailgate.

183 · Sign and carry your organ donor card.

184 · Don't allow self-pity. The moment this emotion strikes, do something nice for someone less fortunate than you.

185 · Don't accept "good enough" as good enough.

186 · Go to a country fair and check out the 4-H Club exhibits. It will renew your faith in the younger generation.

187 · Select a doctor your own age so that you can grow old together.

188 · At the movies, buy Junior Mints and sprinkle them on your popcorn.

189 · Make a list of twenty-five things you want to experience before you die. Carry it in your wallet and refer to it often.

190 · Every person that you meet knows some-thing you don't; learn from them.

191 · Tape record your parents' laughter.

192 • Laugh a lot. A good sense of humor cures almost all of life's ills.

193 • Never underestimate the power of a kind word or deed.

194 • Don't untertip the waiter just because the food is bad; he didn't cook it.

195 · Don't be afraid to say, "I don't know."

196 · Don't be afraid to say, "I made a mistake."

197 · Don't be afraid to say, "I need help."

198 · Don't be afraid to say, "I'm sorry."

199 · Conduct family fire drills. Be sure everyone knows what to do in case the house
catches fire.

200 · Never compromise your integrity.

201 · Keep a note pad and pencil on your bed-
side table. Million-dollar ideas sometimes
strike at 3 A.M.

202 · Show respect for everyone who works for
a living, regardless of how trivial their job.

203 · Send your loved one flowers. Think of a
reason later.

204 · Don't use time or words carelessly.
Neither can be retrieved.

205 · Look for opportunities to make people feel important.

206 · When talking to the press, remember they always have the last word.

207 · When planning a trip abroad, read about the places you'll visit before you go or, better yet, rent a travel video.

208 · Don't rain on other people's parades.

209 · Don't interrupt.

210 · Don't be rushed into making an important decision. People will understand if you say, "I'd like a little more time to think it over. Can I get back to you tomorrow?"

211 · Enjoy real maple syrup.

212 · Before leaving to meet a flight, call the airline first to be sure it's on time.

213 · Be prepared. You never get a second chance to make a good first impression.

214 ᐧ Give thanks before every meal.

215 ᐧ Don't insist on running someone else's life.

216 ᐧ Watch for big problems. They disguise big opportunities.

217 • Get into the habit of putting your billfold and car keys in the same place when entering your home.

218 • Learn a card trick.

219 • Give people the benefit of the doubt.

220 · Never admit at work that you're tired, angry, or bored.

221 · Make someone's day by paying the toll for the person in the car behind you.

222 · Don't make the same mistake twice.

223 · Keep an extra key hidden somewhere on your car in case you lock yourself out.

224 · Never discuss money with people who have much more or much less than you.

225 · Don't be called out on strikes. Go down swinging.

226 · Cherish your children for what they are,
not for what you'd like them to be.

227 · Keep several irons in the fire.

228 · Commit yourself to quality.

229 · Become someone's hero.

230 · Marry only for love.

231 · Count your blessings.

232 · Call your mother.

DREAMS

Compiled by Hy Brett

A FATHER'S PRAYER

Build me a son, O Lord,
who will be strong enough to know
when he is weak, and brave enough to face
himself when he is afraid, one who will be
proud and unbending in honest defeat, and
humble and gentle in victory.

—General Douglas MacArthur

The secret of happiness is not in doing what one likes, but liking what one has to do.

—James M. Barrie

Be glad of life because it gives you the chance to love and to work and to play and to look up at the stars.

—Henry van Dyke

Try not to become a person of success but rather a person of value.

—Albert Einstein

A person is no greater than his or her dreams, ideals, hopes, and plans. A person dreams the dream and dreams of fulfilling it. It's the dream that makes the person.

—Zig Ziglar

Every new life is a new thing under the sun; there has never been anything just like it before, and never will be again. A young man ought to get that idea about himself; he should look for the single spark of individuality that makes him different from other folks, and develop that for all he is worth.

—Henry Ford

Keep away from people who try to belittle your ambitions. Small people always do that, but the really great make you feel that you, too, can become great.

—Mark Twain

Everybody can be great . . . because anybody can serve. You don't have to have a college degree to serve. You don't have to make your subject and verb agree to serve. You only need a heart full of grace. A soul generated by love.

—Martin Luther King, Jr.

God has not left you adrift on a sea of heredity. The past does not have to be your prison. You have a voice in your destiny. You have a say in your life. You have a choice in the path you take.

Choose well and someday—generations from now—your grandchildren and great-grandchildren will thank God for the seeds you sowed.

—Max Lucado (adapted)

Don't aim to be an earthly saint,
With eyes fixed on a star:
Just try to be the fellow that
Your mother thinks you are.

—Will S. Adkin

Be very careful that none under you oppress the people or torment them with vexations. . . . Live in peace and quiet with your neighbors, and know that kings and princes may be as great robbers as thieves and pirates . . . and be not carried away by ambition . . . to enlarge your territories by unjust acquisitions, be content with what is your own.

—King James II of England, to his son Prince James Francis Edward

Let your life dance lightly over the edges of time like dew on the tip of a leaf.

—Rabindranath Tagore

The only moral lesson which is suited for a child, the most important lesson for every time of life, is this: "Never hurt anybody."

—Denis Breeze

Our life is what our thoughts make it.

—Marcus Aurelius

To live is to change, and to be perfect is to have changed often.

—Cardinal John Henry Newman

When a thing is done, it's done. Don't look back. Look forward to your next objective.

—General George C. Marshall

Strong hope is a much greater stimulant of life than any single realized joy could be.

—Friedrich Nietzsche

A FATHER'S ADVICE TO HIS SON

My blessing with thee!
And these few precepts in thy memory
See thou character. Give thy thoughts no tongue,
Nor any unproportion'd thought his act.
Be thou familiar, but by no means vulgar.
Those friends thou hast, and their adoption tried,
Grapple them unto thy soul with hoops of steel;
But do not dull thy palm with entertainment
Of each new-hatch'd, unfledg'd comrade. Beware
Of entrance to a quarrel; but being in,
Bear't that th' opposed may beware of thee.
Give every man thine ear, but few thy voice;
Take each man's censure, but reserve thy judgment.

Costly thy habit as thy purse can buy,
But not express'd in fancy; rich, not gaudy;
For the apparel oft proclaims the man,
And they in France of the best rank and station
Are of a most select and generous chief in that.
Neither a borrower nor a lender be;
For loan oft loses both itself and friend,
And borrowing dulls the edge of husbandry.
This above all: to thine own self be true,
And it must follow, as the night the day,
Thou canst not then be false to any man.
Farewell. My blessing season this in thee!

—Shakespeare, *Hamlet*

If you live without being a father, you will die without being a human being.

—Russian proverb

What a father says to his children is not heard by the world, but it will be heard by posterity.

—John Paul Richter

One should be mentally clear, morally pure, and physically tidy.

—Anton Chekhov

To laugh often and much; to win the respect of intelligent people and the affection of children, to earn the appreciation of honest critics and endure the betrayal of false friends; to appreciate beauty, to find the best in others, to leave the world a bit better whether by a healthy child, a garden patch, or a redeemed social condition; to know even one life has breathed easier because you lived. This is to have succeeded.

—Ralph Waldo Emerson

Happy the man, and happy he alone,

He, who can call today his own;

He who, secure within, can say:

"Tomorrow, do thy worst, for I have lived today.

—Horace

To be happy at home is the ultimate aim of all ambition; the end to which every enterprise and labor tends, and of which every desire prompts the prosecution.

—Samuel Johnson

If one advances confidently in the direction of his dreams and endeavors to live the life which he has imagined, he will meet with a success unexpected in common hours. . . . If you have built castles in the air, your work need not be lost; that is where they should be. Now put the foundations under them.

—Henry David Thoreau

GO FORTH TO LIFE

Go forth to life, oh! child of Earth.
Still mindful of thy heavenly birth;
Thou art not here for ease or sin,
But manhood's noble crown to win.

Though passion's fire are in thy soul,
Thy spirit can their flames control.
Though tempters strong beset thy way,
Thy spirit is more strong than they.

Go on from innocence of youth
To manly pureness, manly truth;
God's angels still are near to save,
And God himself doth help the brave.

Then forth to life, oh! child of Earth,
Be worthy of thy heavenly birth,
For noble service thou art here;
Thy brothers help, thy God revere.

—Samuel Longfellow

Each of us will one day be judged by our standard of life, not by our standard of living; by our measure of giving, not by our measure of wealth; by our simple goodness, not by our seeming greatness.

—William Arthur Ward

Man acquires a particular quality by constantly acting a particular way . . . . We become just by performing just actions, temperate by performing temperate actions, brave by performing brave actions.

—Aristotle

Cherish your visions and your dreams as they are the children of your soul; the blueprints of your ultimate achievements.

—Napoleon Hill

We never reflect how pleasant it is to ask for nothing.

—Seneca

A man's first problem is to find out what kind of work he is to do in the universe.

—Thomas Carlyle

Let nothing foul to either eye or ear reach those doors within which dwells a boy.

—Juvenal

Walking is a man's best medicine.

—Hippocrates

Good nature is more agreeable in conversation than wit and gives a certain air to the countenance which is more amiable than beauty.

—Joseph Addison

Many years ago a shoemaker was teaching his nine-year-old son his craft to prepare him for life. One day, an awl fell from the shoemaker's table and tragically put out his son's eye. Without the medical knowledge and expertise of today, the son ended up losing not only that eye, but the other one as well.

His father put him in a special school for people without sight. At that time they were taught to read by using large carved wooden blocks. The blocks were clumsy, awkward to handle, and required a considerable amount of time to learn. The shoemaker's son, however, was not content only to learn to read. He knew there must be an easier, better way. Over the years, he devised a new reading system for people who were blind by punching dots into paper. To accomplish his objective, the shoemaker's son used the same awl that had blinded him. His name was Louis Braille.

The saying is still true: It's not what happens to you; it's how you handle what happens to you that counts.

—Zig Ziglar (adapted)

The reading of all good books is like a conversation with all the finest men of past centuries.

—René Descartes

Never worry about anything that is past. Charge it up to experience and forget the trouble. There are always plenty of troubles ahead, so don't turn and look back on any behind you.

—Herbert Hoover

Don't just count your years, make your years count.

—Ernest Meyers

PRAYER FOR A SON AT THE JEWISH NEW YEAR

May God bless you and guide you. Be strong for truth, charitable in your words, just and loving in your deeds. A noble heritage has been entrusted to you; guard it well.

May God inspire you to live in the tradition of Ephraim and Menasheh, who carried forward the life of our people.

The Lord bless you and keep you;

The Lord look kindly upon you and be gracious to you;

The Lord bestow His favor upon you and give you peace.

—*Gates of the House: The New Union Home Prayer Book*

To renounce your individuality, to see with another's eyes, to hear with another's ears, to be two and yet but one, to so melt and mingle that you no longer know you are you or another, to constantly absorb and constantly radiate, to reduce earth, sea and sky, and all that is in them to a single being so wholly that nothing whatever is withheld, to be prepared at any moment for sacrifice, to double your personality in bestowing it—that is love.

—Théophile Gautier

When the one man loves the one woman and the one woman loves the one man, the very angels leave heaven and come and sit in that house and sing for joy.

—Brahma

Those who love deeply never grow old; they may die of old age, but they die young.

—Benjamin Franklin

Journeys end in lovers meeting,
Every wise man's son doth know.

—Shakespeare

The sooner this engagement is consummated the better. You say that Sarah possesses every quality necessary to make you happy. . . . You will please communicate to her that you have my full and free consent that you be united in the holy bonds of matrimony; that I shall receive her as a daughter, and cherish her as my child. . . . Present me affectionately to Sarah, for although unknown to me, your attachment has created in my bosom a parental regard for her. That, I have no doubt, will increase upon acquaintance.

—Andrew Jackson, to his adopted son Andrew, Jr.

If I see what I want real good in my mind, I don't notice any pain in getting it.

—George Foreman, when asked how he could stand all the pain it took to become heavyweight champion

There are two things to aim at in life: first, to get what you want; and after that, to enjoy it. Only the wisest of mankind achieve the second.

—Logan Pearsall Smith

Admire people who do great things, even though they fail.

—Seneca

If I had influence with the good fairy who is supposed to preside over the christening of all children, I should ask that her gift to each child in the world be a sense of wonder so indestructible that it would last throughout life.

—Rachel Carson

Serve God; let Him be the author of all thy actions; commend all thy endeavors to Him. Let my experienced advice and fatherly instructions sink deep into thy heart. So God direct thee in all His way, and fill thy heart with his grace.

—Sir Walter Raleigh, to his son Walter, Jr.

One negative outcome to an education is that it enables us to worry more intelligently about global issues and the unpredictable future. That being the case, worry never robs tomorrow of its problems—it only saps today of its strength.

Trade worry time for problem analysis, preparation, prayer, and praise.

—Dianna Booher

I don't care if he grows up to be a Democrat or a Republican, just as long as he's healthy and becomes a starting pitcher for the Mets.

—Leo McCoskey

A man looketh on his little one as a being of better hope; in himself ambition is dead, but it hath a resurrection in his son.

—Martin F. Tupper

A wise man will make more opportunities than he finds.

—Francis Bacon

All fathers entertain the pious wish of seeing their own shortcomings realized in their sons. It is quite as though one could live for a second time and put in full use all the experiences of one's first career.

—Goethe

The best way for a young man who is without friends or influence to begin is: first, to get a position; second, to keep his mouth shut; third, observe; fourth, be faithful; fifth, make his employer think he would be lost in a fog without him; sixth, be polite.

—Russell Sage

A small boy once asked his parents, "I'm going to pray now— do you need anything?" With childlike faith, the boy believed that time spent in prayer would bring about the results he wanted. Somewhere along the road to becoming adults, however, many of us have lost our passion for time alone with God. It's important to recapture that faith and remember that we are not strong enough to carry out life's tough choices alone.

—Todd Duncan (adapted)

I don't know who my grandfather was; I am much more
concerned to know what his grandson will be.

—Abraham Lincoln

To be what we are, and to become what we are capable of
becoming, is the only end of life.

—Robert Louis Stevenson

Best men are often moulded out of faults.

—Shakespeare

Your work was waste? Maybe your share
Lay in the hour you laughed and kissed;
Who knows but that your son may wear
The laurels that his father missed.

—Laurence Hope

Do not worry about your life, what you will eat or what you will drink; nor about your body, what you will put on. Is not life more than food, and the body more than clothing? Look at the birds of the air, for they neither sow nor reap nor gather into barns; yet your heavenly Father feeds them. Are you not of more value than they? Which of you by worrying can add one cubit to his stature?

—Matthew 6:25–27

Far better it is to dare mighty things, to win glorious triumphs, even though checkered with failure, than to take rank with those poor spirits who neither enjoy much nor suffer much because they live in the gray twilight that knows not victory nor defeat.

—Theodore Roosevelt

What is the true measure of success? Your best. Nothing less. In all things, success should be determined by contribution, not accumulation.

—Dianna Booher

It is very easy in the world to live by the opinion of the world. It is very easy in solitude to be self-centered, but the finished man is he who in the midst of the crowd keeps with perfect sweetness the independence of solitude. I knew a man of simple habits and earnest character who never put out his hands nor opened his lips to court the public, and having survived several rotten reputations of young men, Honor came at last and sat down with him upon his private bench from which he had never stirred.

—Ralph Waldo Emerson

The great thing in this world is not so much where we are, but in what direction we are moving.

—Oliver Wendell Holmes

Live your life and forget your age.

—Norman Vincent Peale

Moderation is usually a good thing, but let us remember that Johann Sebastian Bach had twenty-three children, and that four of his sons were great musicians.

—George Bernard Shaw

And oh, my son, by all means keep from the use of tobacco.
Don't smoke or chew. Besides the habit of its use, it is an
expense and trouble. I look to you as one on whom my man-
tle is to fall, and I wish to leave it to you without a rent in it.

—Sam Houston, to his son Sam, Jr.

See, the streams of living waters,
   springing from eternal Love
Well supply thy sons and daughters,
   and all fear of want remove.

—John Newton

A bit of fragrance always clings to the hand that gives you roses.

—Chinese proverb

The sky is the daily bread of the eyes.

—Ralph Waldo Emerson

For the man sound of body and serene of mind there is no such thing as bad weather; every day has its beauty, and storms which whip the blood do but make it pulse more vigorously.

—George Gissing

The wise man does not lay up treasure. The more he gives to others, the more he has for his own.

—Lao-Tse

Human felicity is produced not as much by great pieces of good fortune that seldom happen as by little advantages that occur every day.

—Benjamin Franklin

If you believe—really believe—you will persist.

—Zig Ziglar

You will try to emancipate yourself as much as possible from the thraldom of abject dependence for your daily wants of life on your servants. The more you can do for yourself, the greater will be your independence and real comfort. The Church Catechism has enumerated the duties which you owe to God and your neighbor—let your rule of conduct be always in strict conformity with those precepts, and remember that the first and principal one of all, given us by our Lord and Savior Himself, is this: "that you shall love your neighbor as yourself, and do unto men as you would they should do unto you."

—Queen Victoria and Prince Albert, to their son the Prince of Wales

You cannot teach a child to take care of himself unless you will let him try to take care of himself. He will make mistakes, and out of these mistakes will come his wisdom.

—Henry Ward Beecher

What a large volume of adventures may be grasped within the little span of life, by him who interests his heart in everything, and who, having eyes to see what time and chance are perpetually holding out to him as he journeyeth on his way, misses nothing he can fairly lay his hands on!

—Laurence Sterne

We have not passed that subtle line between childhood and adulthood until we move from the passive voice to the active voice—that is, until we have stopped saying "It got lost," and say, "I lost it."

—Sidney J. Harris

Do not pray for easy lives. Pray to be stronger men. Do not pray for tasks equal to your powers. Pray for powers equal to your tasks.

—Phillips Brooks

Life is a direction, not a destination. All we need to do to live in better times is to change our outlook on the present. Gratitude clears the road noise, cuts through the congestion, and gives us new perspective.

—Dianna Booher

When a resolute young fellow steps up to the great bully, the world, and takes him boldly by the beard, he is often surprised to find it comes off in his hand, and that it was only tied on to scare away timid adventurers.

—Ralph Waldo Emerson

Nothing can be more pleasing to God Almighty and to all good people than that brothers and sisters should love each other, and try to make each other happy, but it is impossible to be happy without being good, and the beginning and the A.B.C. of goodness is to be dutiful and affectionate to their parents; to be obedient to them when they are present, and to pray for them and to write frequent letters from a thankful and loving heart when both or either of them chance to be absent.

—Samuel Taylor Coleridge, to his son Derwent

Love Virtue, she alone is free;
She can teach ye how to climb
Higher than the sphery chime;
Or if Virtue feeble were,
Heaven itself would stoop to her.

—John Milton

Adapt yourself to the things among which your lot has been cast and love sincerely the fellow creatures with whom destiny has ordained that you shall live.

—Marcus Aurelius

Wﾠhat can be added to a man who is in health, out of debt, and has a clear conscience?

—Adam Smith

Dﾠo what you feel in your heart to be right—for you'll be criticized anyway. You'll be damned if you do, and damned if you don't.

—Eleanor Roosevelt

Mﾠy hopes are not always realized, but I always hope.

—Ovid

Happy those who live in the dream of their own existence, and see all things in the light of their own minds; who walk by faith and hope; to whom the guiding star of their youth still shines from afar, and into whom the spirit of the world has not entered.

—William Hazlitt

Be not scurrilous in conversation, nor satirical in thy jests. The one will make thee unwelcome to all company; the other pull on quarrels, and get the hatred of thy best friends.

—William Cecil, Lord Burghley, to his son Robert

I write this note today because your going away is so much upon my mind, and because I want you to have a few parting words from me, to think of now and then at quiet times. I need not tell you that I love you dearly, and am very, very sorry in my heart to part with you. But this life is half made up of parting, and these pains must be borne. . . .

Never take a mean advantage of anyone in a transaction, and never be hard upon people who are in your power. Try to do to others as you would have them do to you, and do not be discouraged if they fail sometimes. It is much better for you that they should fail in obeying the greatest rule laid down by our Savior than that you should.

I put a New Testament among your books for the very same reasons, and with the very same hopes, that made me write an easy account of it for you, when you were a little child. Because it is the best book that ever was, or will be, known in the world; and because it teaches you the best lessons by which any human creature, who tried to be truthful and faithful to duty, can possibly be guided. . . . Never abandon the wholesome practice of saying your own private prayers, night and morning. I have never abandoned it myself, and I know the comfort of it. I hope you will always be able to say in after life that you had a kind father. You cannot show your affection for him so well, or make him so happy, as by doing your duty.

—Charles Dickens, to his son Edward

Take calculated risks. This is quite different from being rash.

—George S. Patton

Do not be too timid and squeamish about your actions. All life is an experiment. The more experiments you make, the better. What if they are a little coarse, and you may get your coat soiled or torn? What if you fail, and get fairly rolled in the dirt once or twice? Up again, you shall never be so afraid of a tumble.

—Ralph Waldo Emerson

To look up and not down,
To look forward and not back,
To look out and not in, and
To lend a hand.

—Edward Everett Hale

You're only young once, but you can be immature forever.

—John Greier

Low company and low pleasures are always more costly than liberal and elegant ones.

—Lord Chesterfield

It is of practical value to learn to like yourself. Since you must spend so much time with yourself you might as well get some satisfaction out of the relationship.

—Norman Vincent Peale

Make a rule and pray to God to help you keep it: never, if possible, lie down at night without being able to say, "I have made one human being a little wiser or a little happier or at least a little better this day."

—Charles Kingsley

If time be of all things most precious, wasting time must be the greatest prodigality, since lost time is never found again; and what we call time enough always proves little enough. Let us then be up and doing, and doing to a purpose; so by diligence shall we do more with less perplexity.

—Benjamin Franklin

Seminary ended. Dad came from Iowa to see me in cap and gown, graduating from my three years of graduate studies.

I was ordained as a preacher in the oldest Protestant denomination in the history of the United States.

And my dad cried.

Finally, twenty years later, he told me why he had cried that morning years ago when I had first told him, "I prayed last night, 'Make me a preacher when I grow up.'"

"Harold, I wanted to be a minister for Jesus Christ when I was a little boy. But my dad and mom died when I was in the sixth grade. I had to quit school and get a job as a farm hand. So I prayed, 'God, make me a minister through one of my sons someday.'

"My first baby was a girl, my second, a boy. He never liked books or school and was destined to be a farmer. The next child was a girl. And the next—our last, we thought—was a girl.

"Many years later your mom got pregnant again. It was a boy. You were born. How I prayed, 'Take him, Lord, and make him your preacher.' But I never, never, never wanted you to know how I felt. It had to be an honest call from the Lord.

"That's why I cried when you told me, 'I'm going to be a preacher when I grow up.' God had answered my childhood prayers, Harold."

We cried and hugged.

—Robert H. Schuller (adapted)

He who is taught to live upon little owes more to his father's wisdom than he who has a great deal left him does to his father's care.

—William Penn

A man who has been the indisputable favorite of his mother keeps for life the feeling of a conqueror, that confidence of success that often induces real success.

—Sigmund Freud

I look upon every day as lost in which I do not make a new acquaintance.

—Samuel Johnson

Among the things you can give and still keep are your word, a smile, and a grateful heart.

—Zig Ziglar

There is only one way to happiness, and that is to cease worrying about things which are beyond the power of our will.

—Epictetus

It is certainly desirable to know the world from observation as well as from books. A careful and accurate observation of men and manners is necessary to correct many erroneous impressions and impositions, to which the young and inexperienced are exposed in their first intercourse with the world. But there is danger on the other hand, that youth and inexperience by launching into the world too early, may imbibe many false and extravagant notions that may prove injurious to them through life. To travel with advantage requires a maturity of understanding and an extensive knowledge of books. Youth is therefore the proper period for study, manhood for traveling and intercourse with mankind. The ardor of youth is apt to place a false estimate on the novelties of the world, and is easily led astray by the achievements of pleasures, and enchanted by the visions of fancy, or the splendor of a deceitful world.

—Stephen Longfellow, to his son
Henry Wadsworth Longfellow

Know the true value of time. Snatch, seize, and enjoy every moment of it. No idleness, no laziness, no procrastination. Never put off till tomorrow what you can do today.

—Lord Chesterfield

He who has a why to live can bear almost any how.

—Friedrich Nietzsche

We are what we repeatedly do. Excellence, then, is not an art but a habit.

—Aristotle

Take all the swift advantage of the hours.

—Shakespeare

Perhaps there is no more important component of character than steadfast resolution. The boy who is going to be a great man, or is going to count in any way in after life, must make up his mind not merely to overcome a thousand obstacles, but to win in spite of a thousand repulses and defeats.

—Theodore Roosevelt

I thought you were disposed to criticize the dress of some of the boys as not so good as your own. Never despite any one for any thing that he cannot help—least of all, for his poverty. I would wish you to keep up appearances yourself as a defense against the idle sneers of the world, but I would not have you value yourself upon them.

—William Hazlitt, to his son William, Jr.

A life is not important except in the impact it has on others.

—Jackie Robinson

Never speak of yourself to others; make them talk about themselves instead; therein lies the whole art of pleasing. Everybody knows it, and everyone forgets it.

—Edmond and Jules de Goncourt

The habit of looking on the best side of every event is worth more than a thousand pounds a year.

—Samuel Johnson

Spend all you have for loveliness,
Buy it and never count the cost;
For one white singing hour of peace
Count many a year of strife well lost,
And for a breath of ecstasy
Give all you have, or could be.

—Sara Teasdale

I must study politics and war that my sons may have liberty to study mathematics and philosophy. My sons ought to study mathematics and philosophy, geography, natural history, naval architecture, navigation, commerce, and agriculture, in order to give their children a right to study painting, poetry, music, architecture, statuary, tapestry, and porcelain.

—John Adams

Do every day or two something for no other reason than you would rather not do it, so that when the hour of dire need draws nigh, it might find you not unnerved and untrained to stand the test.

—William James

Let the counsel of thine own heart stand; for there is no man more faithful unto thee than it. For a man's mind is sometime wont to tell him more than seven watchmen, that sit above in a high tower.

—Ecclesiasticus 37: 13–14

There is a matter which gave me greatest concern when you mentioned it. You said you had put into some lottery for the Derby and had hedged to make it safe. Now all this is bad, bad, nothing but bad. Of all the habits gambling is the one I hated most and have avoided most. Of all habits it grows most on eager minds. Success and loss alike make it grow. . . . Morally it is unchivalrous and unchristian. . . . I have seen many a good fellow ruined by finding himself one day short of money, and trying to get a little by playing or betting—and then the Lord have mercy on his simple soul for simple it will not remain for very long.

Mind, I am not in the least angry with you. Betting is the way of the world. So are all the seven deadly sins under certain rules and pretty names, but to the Devil they lead if indulged in, in spite of the wise world and its ways.

—Reverend Charles Kingsley, to his son

Cheerfulness is the best promoter of health and is as friendly to the mind as to the body.

—Joseph Addison

One must discover oneself. If this does not serve to discover truth, it at least serves as a rule of life and there is nothing better.

—Blaise Pascal

You must do the thing you cannot do.

—Eleanor Roosevelt

I have a dream that my four little children will one day live in a nation where they will not be judged by the color of their skin, but by the content of their character.

—Martin Luther King, Jr.

Most powerful is he who has himself in his own power.

—Seneca

No one ever goes very far unless he accomplishes the impossible at least once a day.

—Elbert Hubbard

Father, O Father! what do we here,
In this land of unbelief and fear;
The Land of Dreams is better far
Above the light of the morning star.

—William Blake

It [marriage] is the most natural state of man, and therefore the state in which you will find solid happiness. . . . It is the man and woman united that makes the complete human being. . . . Together they are most likely to succeed in the world. A single man has not nearly the value he would have in that state of union. He is an incomplete animal. He resembles the odd half of a pair of scissors. If you get a prudent, healthy wife, your industry in your profession, with her good economy, will be a fortune sufficient.

—Benjamin Franklin, to his son William

The secret of happiness is this: Let your interests be as wide as possible, and let your reactions to the things and persons that interest you be as far as possible friendly rather than hostile.

—Bertrand Russell

Nothing is worth more than this day.

—Goethe

The future belongs to those who believe in the beauty of their dreams.

—Eleanor Roosevelt

When you get into a tight place and everything goes against you, till it seems as though you could not hold on a minute longer, never give up then, for that is just the place and time that the tide will turn.

—Harriet Beecher Stowe

One ought never to turn one's back on a threatened danger and try to run away from it. If you do that, you will double the danger. But if you meet it promptly and without flinching, you will reduce the danger by half. Never run away from anything. Never!

—Winston Churchill

This is Daddy's bedtime secret for today. Man is born broken. He lives by mending. The grace of God is glue.

—Eugene O'Neill

God almighty first planted a garden; and, indeed, it is the purest of human pleasures.

—Francis Bacon

To be ignorant of what occurred before you were born is to remain always a child.

—Cicero

IF

If you can keep your head when all about you
　　Are losing theirs and blaming it on you;
If you can trust yourself when all men doubt you,
　　But make allowance for their doubting too:
If you can wait and not be tired by waiting,
　　Or, being lied about, don't deal in lies,
Or being hated don't give way to hating,
　　And yet don't look too good, nor talk too wise;
If you can dream—and not make dreams your master;
　　If you can think—and not make thoughts your aim,
If you can meet with Triumph and Disaster
　　And treat those two impostors just the same:
If you can bear to hear the truth you've spoken
　　Twisted by knaves to make a trap for fools,
Or watch the things you gave your life to, broken,
　　And stoop and build 'em up with worn-out tools;

If you can make one heap of all your winnings
    And risk it on one turn of pitch-and-toss,
And lose, and start again at your beginnings,
    And never breathe a word about your loss:
If you can force your heart and nerve and sinew
    To serve your turn long after they are gone,
And so hold on when there is nothing in you
    Except the Will which says to them: "Hold on!"
If you can talk with crowds and keep your virtue,
    Or walk with Kings—nor lose the common touch,
If neither foes nor loving friends can hurt you,
    If all men count with you, but none too much:
If you can fill the unforgiving minute
With sixty seconds' worth of distance run,
Yours is the Earth and everything that's in it,
And—which is more—you'll be a Man, my son!

                              —Rudyard Kipling

To understand your parents' love you must raise children yourself.

—Chinese proverb

Play no favorites: when Joseph got a many-colored coat, his brothers came to hate him.

—The Midrash

A man's first care should be to avoid the reproaches of his own heart, and his next to escape the censures of the world.

—Joseph Addison

It is almost the definition of a gentleman to say that he is one who never inflicts pain.

—Cardinal John Henry
Newman

It's not how much we have, but how much we enjoy what we have, that makes for happiness.

—Charles Spurgeon

Continue to cultivate a taste for correctness in everything that comes from your pen. A man's future has sometimes been made by his letters' being seen by persons of judgment, and on the contrary many men have lost their characters for good sense and education from the same cause. Never write in a hurry. Even a common note upon the most common business should be written as if it were one day to be read in court or published in a newspaper.

—Dr. Benjamin Rush, to his son James

Hope is the companion of power, and mother of success; for who so hopes strongly has within him the gift of miracles.

—Samuel Smiles

We must accept finite disappointment, but never lose infinite hope.

—Martin Luther King, Jr.

What the best and wisest parent wants for his own child, that must the community want for all its children.

—John Dewey

We never know how high we are
Till we are called to rise.
And then, if we are true to plan,
Our statures touch the skies.

—Emily Dickinson

It is of no consequence of what parents a man is born, as long as he is a man of merit.

—Horace

Great hopes make great men.

—Thomas Fuller

Unblessed is the son who does not honor his parents; but if he is reverent and obedient to them, he will receive the same from his own children.

—Euripides

The mind never need stop growing. Indeed, one of the few experiences which never pall is the experience of watching one's own mind and how it produces new interests, responds to new stimuli, and develops new thoughts, apparently without effort and almost independently of one's own conscious control.

—Gilbert Highet

The important thing in life is to have a great aim and to possess the aptitude and the perseverance to attain it.

—Goethe

You gain strength, courage, and confidence by each experience in which you really stop to look fear in the face. You are able to say to yourself, "I have lived through this horror. I can take the next thing that comes along."

—Eleanor Roosevelt

Don't worry too much about the ultimate meaning of life and why you have particular problems. When a problem arises, ask yourself what's so hard about it and why can't you overcome it. Don't dwell on past failures or the possibility of failure now.

—Marcus Aurelius

Have courage for the great sorrows of life and patience for the small ones; and when you have laboriously accomplished your daily task, go to sleep in peace. God is awake.

—Victor Hugo

Possessions, outward success, publicity, luxury—to me these have always been contemptible. I assume that a simple and unassuming manner of life is best for everyone, best for both the body and the mind.

—Albert Einstein

It is a vulgar, ordinary saying, but it is a very true one, that one should always put the best foot forward. One should please, shine, and dazzle, whenever it is possible. . . . Practice all the arts that ever coquette did, to please; be alert and indefatigable in making every man admire, and every woman in love with you. I can tell you, too, that nothing will carry you higher in the world.

—Lord Chesterfield, to his son Philip

When (not if) troubles come your way, remember that the only way to the mountaintop is through the valley.

—Zig Ziglar

The hell to be endured hereafter, of which theology tells, is no worse than the hell we make for ourselves in this world by habitually fashioning our characters in the wrong way.

—William James

The dutifulness of children is the foundation of all virtues.

—Cicero

I do not absolutely condemn shooting, even in a clergyman, though I think it much better that he should not indulge in it; as I know, from inquiry and observations, that it gives great offense to many people. This being the case, I think it desirable that a young man intended for Holy Orders should not acquire a taste for it, which may sometimes be a temptation to him afterwards; and, generally speaking, it is better that the sons of clergymen should be very guarded in their pursuits and amusements, and especially the sons of bishops, who are always watched with a jealous and often with an unfriendly eye.

—Charles James Blomfield, bishop of London, to his son

You don't raise heroes, you raise sons. And if you treat them like sons, they'll turn out to be heroes, even if it's just in your own eyes.

—Walter Schirra, Sr.

The most important thing a father can do for his children is to love their mother.

—Theodore M. Hesburgh

Children are apt to live up to what you believe of them.

—Lady Bird Johnson

Your children will see what you're all about by what you live rather than what you say.

—Wayne Dyer

The most important thing that parents can teach their children is how to get along without them.

—Frank A. Clark

We must teach our children to dream with their eyes open.

—Harry Edwards

When you put faith, hope and love together, you can raise positive kids in a negative world.

—Zig Ziglar

The best inheritance a parent can give his children is a few minutes of his time each day.

—Orlando A. Battista

Lives of great men all remind us
We can make our lives sublime,
And, departing, leave behind us
Footprints on the sands of time

—Henry Wadsworth Longfellow

If you raise your children to feel that they can accomplish any goal or task they decide upon, you will have succeeded as a parent and you will have given your children the greatest of all blessings.

—Brian Tracy

Look up, laugh loud, talk big, keep the color in your cheek and the fire in your eye, adorn your person, maintain your health, your beauty and your animal spirits.

—William Hazlitt

Realize that disappointment may simply be a turn in the road before you see the finish line. The truth is, most delights are sweeter after passing through disappointments along the way. It also helps to remember that getting what you expected may not be what you really wanted.

—Dianna Booher

My dear son, I shall die happy if I know that you are an earnest student of philosophic themes. Do cultivate all the religious emotions, reverence, awe and aspiration, if for no better reason than as a means of self-culture. Read poetry and learn the secret of tears and ecstasy. Go to Catholic and Episcopal churches and surrender yourself to the inspiration of soul-inspiring religious music.

—David G. Croly, to his son Herbert David

Consider well the proportions of things. It is better to be a young June-bug than an old bird of paradise.

—Mark Twain

A long life may not be good enough, but a good life is long enough.

—Benjamin Franklin

The pessimist sees difficulty in every opportunity. The optimist sees the opportunity in every difficulty.

—Winston Churchill

There's no point in being grown-up if you can't be childish sometimes.

—Dr. Who

GOOD AND BAD CHILDREN

Children, you are very little,
And your bones are very brittle;
If you would grow great and stately,
You must try to walk sedately.
You must still be bright and quiet,
And content with simple diet;
And remain, through all bewild'ring,
Innocent and honest children.
Happy hearts and happy faces,
Happy play in grassy places—

That was how in ancient ages,
Children grew to kings and sages.
But the unkind and the unruly,
And the sort who eat unduly,
They must never hope for glory—
Theirs is quite a different story!
Cruel children, crying babies,
All grow up as geese and gabies,
Hated, as their age increases,
By their nephews and their nieces.

—Robert Louis Stevenson

Fate gives us the hand, and we play the cards.

—Arthur Schopenhauer

If a man does not make new acquaintances as he advances through life, he will soon find himself alone. A man, Sir, should keep his friendship in constant repair.

—Samuel Johnson

My father always used to say that when you die, if you've got five real friends, you've had a great life.

—Lee Iacocca

Strive not for gold, for greedy fools
    Measure themselves by poor men never;
Their standard still being richer men,
    Makes them poor ever.
Train up thy mind to feel content,
    What matters then how low thy store?
What we enjoy, and not possess,
    Makes rich or poor.

—W. H. Davies

In America any boy may become President, and I suppose it's just one of the risks he takes.

—Adlai Stevenson

Slumber not in the tents of your fathers. The world is advancing. Advance with it.

—Giuseppe Mazzini

The happiest moments of my life have been the few I have passed at home in the bosom of my family.

—Thomas Jefferson

Inspiration comes of working every day.

—Charles Baudelaire

Thank God every morning when you get up that you have something to do which must be done, whether you like it or not. Being forced to work, and forced to do your best, will breed in you temperance, self-control, diligence, strength of will, content, and a hundred other virtues which the idle never know.

—Charles Kingsley

No man is really happy without a hobby and it makes precious little difference what the outside interest may be—botany, beetles or butterflies; roses, tulips or irises; fishing, mountaineering or antiquities—anything will do so long as he straddles a hobby and rides it hard.

—Sir William Ogler

A day spent without the sight or sound of beauty, the contemplation of mystery, or the search of truth or perfection is a poverty-stricken day; and a succession of days is fatal to human life.

—Lewis Mumford

Far away there in the sunshine are my highest aspirations. I may not reach them, but I can look up and see their beauty, believe in them, and try to follow where they lead.

—Louisa May Alcott

Unless each day can be looked back upon by an individual as one in which he has had some fun, some joy, some real satisfaction, that day is a loss. It is un-Christian and wicked, in my opinion, to allow such a thing to occur.

—Dwight D. Eisenhower

You are unreasonable in expecting to know the sense of your existence. Nobody knows the meaning of any existence—of flower, beast, man, nation, or world. Live each day usefully, innocently and happily as you can, and leave the rest to God. It is time you were married. You are too solitary.

—Charles William Eliot, president of Harvard,
to his son Sam

I don't know what your destiny will be, but one thing I know: the only ones among you who will be really happy are those who will have sought and found how to serve.

—Albert Schweitzer

You are rich though you do not know it. You have wells of kindness within your heart. At times men will bless you more for a smile, a kindly glance, a gesture of forgiveness, than for treasures of gold.

—Abraham Abba Kabak

God grant me the serenity
To accept the things I cannot change,
The courage to change the things I can;
And the wisdom to know the difference.

—Reinhold Niebuhr

There is more to your life than you ever thought. There is more to your story than what you have read. There is more to your song than what you have sung. A good author saves the best for last. A great composer keeps his finest for the finish. And God, the author of life and composer of hope, has done the same for you.

—Max Lucado (adapted)

There are only two lasting bequests we can hope to give to our children. One of these is roots, the other wings.

—Hodding Carter

Live all you can; it's a mistake not to. It doesn't so much matter what you do in particular so long as you have your life. If you haven't had that, what have you had?

—Henry James

You may never have thought of your
dreams as children, but that's what they
are. They are your offspring—the joy of
your today and the hope of your future.
Protect them. Feed them. Nurture them.
Encourage them to grow. Care for them.
For someday, they may take care of you.

—John C. Maxwell